SPEAK UNTIL
SOMEONE
LISTENS

LATRICIA BROWN

Speak Until Someone Listens

Copyright © 2024 by Latricia Brown

Published by BrownStone Literary Publications
Latriciabc@gmail.com
Facebook: Speak Until Someone Listens

Sensitive Contents Alert!
This story discusses events that are very serious and sensitive in nature and may cause an emotional response.

Book Layout and Design
DHBonner Virtual Solutions, LLC
www.dhbonner.net

ISBN for paperback: 979-8-218-58113-8

Printed in the United States of America

This book is dedicated to victims of abuse.
You have a voice, and I encourage you to find yours...
and use it. Speak until someone listens!

TABLE OF CONTENTS

SPECIAL ACKNOWLEDGMENT

To my mother, who provides support of my work! For being my cheerleader and encouraging me in everything I do... *Thank you!*

And, to my husband, for listening to this story over and over again as I wrote each phase of this book!

INTRODUCTION

Bruised, bloody, desperate, and afraid, Lizzy's mother had just barely escaped death at the hands of her abuser. Lizzy's mom and dad met in high school and married during their senior year. Happy and in love, Lizzy's mom desired to make a warm, happy home for her husband and their children to come. Soon, they started having babies—five beautiful daughters. Eventually, what Lizzy's mother thought was a happy home turned into a complete house of terror. Lizzy's father seemed to grow angrier and more aggressive with the birth of each baby. It didn't take long before the fighting began.

Arduous years of sodomy and physical abuse finally exploded the night that Lizzy's father came home and took his anger out on everyone in the house, children included. He yelled at everyone. When Lizzy's mother asked him to calm down, his rage erupted into physical violence; he began flipping tables, breaking glass, and throwing anything he got his hands on. Everyone was afraid, crying, and trying to hide when he started threatening to kill everyone in the house. Lizzy's mother screamed for the children to get out of the house and run next door to the neighbor's house.

As the children scattered about trying to get out of the house, their father grabbed their mother, beating her with closed fists. She fought back as best she could, but it further angered him. To keep her from fighting back, he relentlessly continued beating her into unconsciousness. Dragging her through the house and into their bedroom, he threw her into the wall, where she ultimately landed on the floor. Hitting the floor awakened her. Unable to move, she immediately thought, *Oh my God! He's going to get his weapon!*

When he tried running past her body in the direction of the safe where the weapon was locked away, she extended her leg out, tripping him. He fell, hitting his head on the corner of the large wooden chest in their bedroom, knocking him unconscious. That's when she shrieked through tears, "Please!" "Help me!" She was hysterical but still couldn't move. "Don't leave me!" she shouted, growing weaker and weaker.

Lizzy and her sisters were still trying to reach the front door when they heard their mother cry for help. They were all afraid, but the courage to rescue their mother was stirred up. Unsure of what they would find upon sight, they ran in the direction they heard their mom crying out. Once they located her in her bedroom, they saw their father lying unconscious. Without any thought, they rushed over to help their mother, using every ounce of strength they had to pull her to her feet. They began dragging her through the house and out the door, running for their lives with nothing but the clothes on their backs in the dead of night.

Mother was bloody and barely able to speak or see through her blood-covered eyes. She and her children ran to their next-door neighbor's house, banging on the door. When the neighbor opened the door, Lizzy's mother collapsed into the house right into her neighbor's arms, screaming hysterically. Aware of the history of violence, no questions asked, the neighbor and his wife quickly loaded them all into his car, taking them straight to the local police station. A report was made, and police were immediately dispatched to the house to arrest Lizzy's father. Police took the family to the hospital, where they were interviewed and examined by doctors and social workers.

Lizzy's grandmother was notified and rushed to the hospital immediately. Whenever Lizzy's grandmother received calls such as this one, she always had the same feeling of panic. Grandmother had often warned Lizzy's mother about marrying any man with a quick temper. She always warned that Lizzy's father was a ticking timebomb just waiting to explode, but Lizzy's mom was a hopeless romantic. She did not heed the warnings. In fact, she did the complete opposite. Mother brushed grandmother's warnings aside, saying that grandmother was older and had gotten bitter because she never found a man to love her the way good men should love their women. Lizzy's mom vowed to prove her mother's view about men and relationships wrong.

Arresting Lizzy's father got him out of the house for good because, eventually, he was given a very lengthy prison sentence. Lizzy and her sisters would be young adults by the time their father would be released from prison. His prison sentence gave Lizzy's mother much-needed time and space, allowing her a chance to reflect and think wisely about choosing a life of peace without being abused. The divorce soon followed, opening the door to freedom for the family.

Close to four years later, the family had settled into a new life. Lizzy's mother was happy. She had finally gotten over the relationship with her ex-husband, Lizzy's father. She had even begun working a lucrative job to make ends meet. This is where she met Jim, whom she would eventually marry.

As it would turn out, Lizzy would become her stepfather's target for abuse. At the innocent age of eight years old, Lizzy suffered from sexual, physical, and emotional abuse at the hands of her new stepfather, Jim. She had nobody she was comfortable enough with to report this abuse to. Lizzy reported several incidents to her mom and even her grandmother, the two people she thought she could trust and confide in. Yet they rejected her reports of abuse—her mother repeatedly warning her to stop flouncing around her stepfather, enticing him, and blaming her for every beating and every rape she suffered at the hands of her stepfather, who alienated Lizzy and the rest of her siblings from their friends and other family members. He even forced them to distrust each other. Eventually, Lizzy fell into depression and saw no way out of this situation.

One day, after many years of suffering, when Lizzy became a teenager, she finally found the nerve to share the years of abuse with one of her teachers. Will her teacher believe her and help her out of the situation?

Turn the page... and read on.

ONE

In a fit of uncontrolled rage, he grabbed my face and forced me to look into his eyes while he lay on top of me, savagely raping me. He growled in my ears, "You gon' pay for running yo mouth to your crazy ass mother again! She don't give a fuck about you!"

I tried desperately to turn my face to the right so that at least I didn't have to look into his crazed eyes while being forced to endure his savage attack yet again. Tears began streaming down my face as I listened to him tell me that I was nothing but filthy, rotten, dirty trash that nobody loved or even cared about. "Girl, you invisible!" "You a nobody!" "Don't nobody care nothin' about you!"

I could feel my insides ripping. I tried screaming out in pain, but he violently gripped my mouth and chin to keep me quiet. I continued trying to move my face away from his, but he scolded me. "Don't fight me!" he said, riding me harder and harder. Finally, he grunted as he finished. I could smell him as his sweat dripped onto my face and body. He slapped me across my face so hard that I could hear ringing in my ears, making me dizzy.

Now, the tears freely poured from my eyes, and blood gushed out of my mouth. Scared to move, I lay there in my dark room, feeling hopeless. I was afraid, cold, and broken. Once he left, I ran to the bathroom. I didn't recognize myself when I looked in the mirror. The image that stared back at me was so frightening that it made me sick to my stomach. My face was swollen, and my mouth was bloody. I felt dirty, sticky, and wet.

As I showered, blood was running down my legs, coming from my vagina. The pain I was feeling was so intense I could barely move. Once I saw all of the blood coming from everywhere, I panicked and started scrubbing my face and body so hard that my skin began to burn. Tired, I just stood under the running water, barely able to move. This was by far the worst experience I'd ever encountered in my life.

I had cried to my mother countless times before about his random attacks, but my mother blatantly called me a liar. She confidently and boldly denied that he would ever do such a thing. My mother's denial of everything this monster did, even when performed right to her face, made things worse for me. For some reason, she allowed his abuse to continue as if she did not recognize what he was doing, which only allowed him to become more reckless and violent.

I was confused. I knew his actions were wrong, so I couldn't understand why my mother allowed him to do what he was doing. This latest attack had left visible bruises covering my face, and she could see that I was barely able to move, yet still denied that he would ever hurt me. Instead of standing firm against him to protect her children, she became weaker with time.

"You deserve to be punished, Lizzy! You never listen!" she screamed. "Your actions caused all of this drama!" Grabbing my arm and pulling me into my bedroom, my mother warned me that I better not open my mouth about this to anybody, telling me that *whatever happens in her house better stay in her house!*

As my mother pushed me onto my bed, she continued yelling. "Lizzy! You're trying to ruin our family! I won't let anybody ruin my family, not even you!" She stated that nobody would understand why my stepfather punishes us in the manner that he does, even conjuring up tears. But as quickly as the tears fell, she began accusing me again, blaming the entire situation on me.

Before leaving my room for the night, she told me she didn't want to hear anything else about what had just happened. I assured her I wouldn't say anything to anyone, promising her I would keep quiet and do my best to stay out of Jim's way. For reasons I could not understand, I started to believe that maybe this was my fault. It would keep peace if I could just be invisible, not talk at all, be friendly, and be funny. Maybe if I tiptoed around the house, staying out of his way, he wouldn't get so angry with me. Even though I tried my best, my best didn't work! His brutal assaults persisted!

My mother had met Jim at work. When he first came to our house, he took a special liking to me, making me feel so special. I remember him smiling at me and telling me how beautiful I was. Out of the five of us, he picked me as the object of his focus. He even gave me a nickname. "I'm gone call you Lizzy! It's something real *special* about you."

Whenever we went out to eat, he would arrange our seating so I would sit right next to him—between him and my mother. When the waiter came to our table to take our order, he'd beckon me to place mine first. At only eight years old, I never thought, even for one second, about how his attention may have made my sisters feel or even my mother. I didn't realize that this man had plans for me. I only knew I was *special* in the eyes of my new father figure, who showered me with the attention and affection I had never received from anyone else.

After briefly dating Jim, my mother moved him into our peaceful home, and in time, I came to realize that Jim had been making me feel comfortable with intentions to make me his victim. I had become so comfortable with him that his actions confused me. On the one hand, I was angry because I knew he was wrong, but on the other, I felt guilty about being angry with him. It seemed like he had multiple personalities that would change without warning. I couldn't figure him out, so I tried to stay out of his way. This didn't always work either because even when I was tucked away in my bedroom, sometimes he would bolt through my door in a rage.

Confusion plagued me because I couldn't keep him happy. Keeping him happy would make all of this go away. Or so I thought. I wanted to do everything I could to keep him happy so he wouldn't attack me. Eventually, I quit trying because nothing I did satisfied him. I finally understood that he was just who he was: a monster! Finally, realizing that I was powerless, I gave up speaking to my mother about what my stepfather was doing to me.

At times, I even packed a small bag, thinking I could just run away from home. The only thing was, I had nowhere to go. So, I decided to do whatever it took to survive this ordeal, to figure out ways to escape this terror... now that our once-happy home would become sad and distressed for the next eight years.

TWO

ON THE FIRST day of his move into our home, he sanctioned a "family" meeting, which included my mother, me, and my sisters. Through gritted teeth and tight lips, he angrily expelled a list of changes he required us to make immediately, or we would face harsh consequences.

Some of his changes were unreasonable and didn't make logical sense. My judgment of him was instantly validated as I quickly discovered his motives. Every change he made was to ultimately benefit his sexual appetite, predatory behavior, and desire for children. One rule was that we were no longer permitted to close the door to our bedrooms, even when occupied. Knowing that we didn't want him to see us while we were dressing ourselves, we would have to quietly listen to hear if he was even remotely in the area of the house near our bedrooms. If he were not, then we would quickly get dressed. Although we could close the bathroom door when we occupied it, we could no longer lock it whenever we used it.

We used to freely use our front door to enter and exit our home. Well, even this changed! We were now required to walk past our front door straight to the rear of the house to enter and exit using the back door. What caused concern for all of us was that he brought an adult German Shepherd dog with him that now occupied our backyard. Every time we approached the rear of our home, his dog growled and barked at us through seething teeth.

Additionally, we needed permission to listen to music on the record player we used to listen to every day before he came to live with us. It was now taboo for us to even look in the direction of the record player. Because of Jim, music seemed to have lost the meaning it once had for us. It no longer sounded the same. Nor were we allowed to watch television. So, for the years he lived in our house, we lost sight of all of our childhood television shows—even cartoons that came on every Saturday morning.

He even prohibited us from going outside to sit on our porch; therefore, interactions with our friends came to an immediate halt. At times, he even prevented us from talking to each other. I remember him questioning me and my sisters about our conversations. It appeared that his goal was to alienate us from everything and everyone we knew, even each other, and it worked! We all became afraid to talk to each other.

Until he entered our home, we lived freely, enjoying each other to the fullest with lots of love and laughter. Although my mother was a single parent and there was a financial struggle, we were happy. I vividly remember my sisters and I snuggling with my mother in her bed at night, watching scary movies and eating Chinese food. We laughed together a lot! Trying to imitate our beautiful mother, we would put on her clothes and shoes, play in her make-up, and sashay around the house, carrying her purses. Sometimes, we would play jacks, and almost every weekend, my mother would take us roller skating, bowling, or to the local movie theater downtown.

Whatever the event, my mother was an active participant. She taught us to dance and skate. She loved music, so we always played the latest songs on our record player. Believe it or not, our friends pinned my mother the "cool" mother. Everyone thought our house was the "Fun House" because my mother was so fun to be around. She was young, beautiful, and loved having a good time with us. I had many lovely memories in our home with my mother and sisters. Before he came, that is...

When she first started bringing him to our home to visit, I thought his presence was ominous. I couldn't explain what I felt whenever he was around; I just knew I didn't get a good feeling from him. I snuffed at my own intuition because he had made me feel so special. He was always smiling and winking at me. Jim was easy-going, but he seemed evil.

Looking back, now I understand why I had eerie feelings about him. He was a complete monstrous predator.

From a young age, I had the ability to discern people. Everyone seemed so predictable. I would observe everyone in my presence when they were smiling because eyes generally don't lie. Looking at Jim whenever we talked, I could see evil behind his eyes, even through his smile. His facial expressions did not match the words he spoke or his laugh. One evening, when my mother was out with him, my sisters and I were talking. I brought up how I felt, and my oldest sister agreed that he was weird. However, she couldn't identify anything in particular about him to rightfully accuse him.

* * *

I remember the next attack like it was yesterday. Soon, I realized why Jim no longer wanted us to lock the bathroom door while we occupied it. He wanted easy access to us. One day, while taking a bath, my instinct told me to close the shower curtains. As I was rinsing off, I heard someone walk into the bathroom. I froze. My heart was beating like a drum, and I didn't know what to do, so I simply stood—frozen in silence.

As footsteps approached the bathtub, I felt scared and helpless, quickly grabbing my towel and wrapping it around my body as he snatched the shower curtains open. I looked up at him as his eyes scoured my body up and down. He stood there for what seemed like hours. Finally, he ordered me to hang the towel back on the towel rack.

When I hesitated, he mistook my delay for being disrespectful, so he snatched the towel from me and slapped me so hard that I temporarily lost vision in my left eye and heard ringing in my left ear. I slipped down into the water and started to cry out, not knowing how to get myself out of the situation. My crying seemed to snap him back to reality because he left me alone... that time. When he left the bathroom, he muttered something I could not hear clearly.

Sitting in the water, afraid to move, I could feel the left side of my face stinging and beginning to swell. Continuing to cry, I dried myself off, thinking to myself, even as young as I was, that this monster wanted to harm me. Being a child, I didn't comprehend the brevity of what kind of harm he intended. I just knew he meant harm. Before finally leaving the bathroom, I poked my head into the hallway to see if anyone else, especially him, was nearby. I felt somewhat safe when I saw that nobody else was around. I quickly scurried across the hall to my bedroom, shut the door, slid down the wall onto the floor, curled up into a ball, and exhaled.

A tidal wave of tears began flowing steadily at that point, but then I remembered I would be faced with harsh consequences if he caught me with my bedroom door closed. While crying, I jumped to my feet and opened the bedroom door, looking around to make sure he wasn't around.

I was in total disbelief but didn't utter a word to anyone.

Later that night, at dinner, my mother looked at me with pain in her eyes. She could see that my face was bruised. I thought, *surely, she will do something to help us escape our monster*. When she asked me what had happened to my face, Jim quickly exclaimed, "She was running her mouth again! I gave her what she's been asking for!" My mother looked down at her plate of food as if unbothered by his response.

My oldest sister and I locked eyes. She knew exactly what had happened. I saw hurt in her eyes, which watered as she picked at her food. We were completely broken.

THREE

At this point, I was nine years old and had never actually talked about this abuse to my sisters, wondering if the same thing was happening to them. Nobody was talking about it.

I did notice a change in my sisters and my mother. Everyone, including my mother, transitioned from being happy, cheerful, and outgoing to being sad and withdrawn most of the time. None of us talked anymore. We all walked on eggshells... each one of us was a nervous wreck—always on edge.

This monster left home for a few hours on a rare occasion. So, one day, after realizing he was gone, I went to my mother. She sat quietly, reading as she always did in the early evenings. I didn't know how to approach her because I was afraid. At the last minute, I hesitated and turned to scurry back into my bedroom.

"Lizzy! Lizzy! Come here for one moment!"

My mother was calling out to me. Taking a deep breath in, not knowing what she was going to say, I walked back to her. She held her arms up, reaching for me, welcoming me to sit with her. I sat down, and the tears just poured from my soul. She grabbed me and hugged me tightly. I began exhaling all of my anxiety, fears, and frustration through my tears; I felt safe, momentarily feeling the security I used to feel from her before Jim, the monster, moved into our home.

For a moment, no words were exchanged. Then, my mother began to cry, too, saying, "Oh, Lizzy, It's not so bad! You've got to figure out what you're doing to make him angry!"

Frustrated with her words, I couldn't wrap my mind around what she was saying. I hadn't done anything to deserve this, but the only words I could muster were, "But Ma, he hurts me for no reason!" I expected her response to be understanding, belief in me, and anger towards him. Instead, she shook her head no and said, "No! He would never..." Just as she began talking, we heard the door lock turning to indicate that he was entering back into the house. My face and clothing saturated with tears, I quickly ran back into my bedroom, feeling defeated, helpless, and hopeless.

From my room, I could see my mother's face. She tried hard not to appear upset or disheveled. She must have pulled it off because he never questioned her. I just wished I could have spoken more clearly to her about what he was doing to me. Maybe if I had, she would have believed me.

Lying in bed that night, I began thinking about who I could trust with my troubles. Sadly, I couldn't think of anyone. I could hear Jim and my mother arguing about something. She kept saying, "No! No! Jim! You're taking this too far!"

I must have dozed off to sleep because I was awakened by Jim snatching me up and pulling me out of bed. Protesting, "No! Stop it!" I tried fighting him, but he was able to overpower me.

"Here! Put this on now!" He barked.

As I shook my head, he tore my pajamas off of me and said, "I said put this on now!" Not knowing why he had woken me up so late at night wanting me to put on shorts and a T-shirt that weren't mine was disorienting. Once I had reluctantly slipped into the clothes he'd given me, he said, "Let's go!" As he was dragging me through the house past my mother, she turned away. Even while I screamed for help, she never looked in my direction. I couldn't believe that my mother could ignore me, her own child, who was in distress.

After Jim put me in my mother's car, we began a long ride through the city, driving past liquor stores and gas stations. This side of town was unfamiliar to me. Many young men and women in their late teens and early twenties stood around talking and smoking. I even saw a group of men who appeared to be rolling dice in a gas station parking lot. My mind was racing, and my heart beat one million times per minute. The streets became even darker once we entered a residential neighborhood because only a few streetlights worked.

Finally, we made it to our destination. "Get out!" Jim said, ordering me out of the car. He noticed that I was reluctant. I wasn't moving fast enough for him, so he rushed around to my door, snatched it open, grabbed my arm, yanked me out of the car, and dragged me to one of only three houses on the block that wasn't boarded up. It appeared to be abandoned. Jim only had to knock a few times before a tall, medium-built, rough-looking man who looked to be in his early twenties wearing a bandana on his head, a wife-beater T-shirt, and jeans opened the door. This man had a drink in his hand and a blunt hanging from his mouth.

"Here she is, man," Jim said, pushing into the house. "You got one hour!"

The man violently grabbed Jim with one hand by his shirt, pulling him close and yelling in his face, "You don't tell me how long I got! I got as long as I need! Get the fuck out of here!"

"Wait!" I screamed, "Where are you going? Why am I here? Take me home... Please!"

But my pleas fell on deaf ears because Jim was long gone. Without saying anything to me, the man led me into a bedroom, and before I could ask any questions, he pushed me down onto the bed and began tearing my clothes off. This is when I realized that I was here for this man's sexual pleasure. As a nine-year-old, I was in bed with a grown man pouncing on me, and I didn't know why. After what seemed like forever, the man fell asleep. I just lay there scared, curled up in a fetal position.

After more time passed, Jim returned. Someone let him into the bedroom, and all he said was, "Let's go!" I never thought I would be happy to see this man. The clothes I had come in had been ripped off of me. Looking around, I saw a large button-up shirt on the bedpost. Putting it around my body to cover up, I darted out of bed and followed Jim back to my mother's car.

The ride home was quiet and miserable for me. Jim never said a word. He wouldn't even look at me. My mother was standing in the doorway as we made it home, but she had disappeared once we walked through the door. I ran straight to the bathroom and let the tears flow as I scrubbed my body as hard as I could while trying to figure out what had happened. *Why had Jim taken me to this man for sex?*

I was relieved that this was one night Jim had actually given me a break! He didn't come into my room that night at all. My momentary sense of relief was soon exchanged for worry as I started thinking about my sisters. Did he go into their rooms instead?

FOUR

THE FOLLOWING DAY IN SCHOOL, I felt so tired. I was angry, confused, and lonely. There was absolutely nobody to talk to. Being withdrawn, I'd never made friends with anyone. Even though nobody disliked or bullied me, I still hadn't made any friends. One day, while my teacher, Mrs. Cunningham, was at the board teaching, my attention was drawn to my inner thoughts. I was trying to think of at least one person I could confide in.

Suddenly, the thought occurred: Maybe I could talk to Mrs. Cunningham about this. Perhaps she could help me sort all of this out. I started thinking of the right time to catch her to talk. Nervous and on edge, my mind raced like a galloping horse. Then, reality hit, *Sharing this with Mrs. Cunningham could never be an option! What if she doesn't believe me?*

"Elizabeth! Are you okay?" Mrs. Cunningham asked.

"I've been calling your name for the answer. Please answer the question!"

I couldn't answer the question because I did not know what the discussion was about. So, instead of answering the question, I quickly responded, "Ah, I-I need help, Mrs. Cunningham!"

Mrs. Cunningham began breaking down the problem for me in terms she thought I could understand. When I was able to complete the problem, she said, "There! You got it... Great job, Elizabeth!"

Realizing that I couldn't share my ordeal with Mrs. Cunningham in front of everyone, at the end of the school day, I created the opportunity to speak with her alone. At the last minute, I lingered around class after it was dismissed. Maybe Mrs. Cunningham would notice my presence and ask if I was okay. Tidying up my desk area, I pretended to be looking for a lost book.

"Elizabeth, come on out!" Mrs. Cunningham said. "It's time to go on home now!"

I was right on the edge of asking her to listen to me when my nerves got the best of me, and I simply decided to leave. I had lingered around so long that by the time I made it to my locker, everyone else had pretty much cleared out of the building except for some school staff. I didn't know any of them, so I knew talking to them was impossible.

Walking home from school, frustration with myself ensued. My thoughts plummeted into a deep, dark tunnel of fear and sadness. I had missed yet another opportunity to tell someone about being abused by my stepfather. I just needed the right person to trust to share my horror story with. I was so immersed in my whirlwind of thoughts that I didn't realize I'd walked right past my house.

I snapped back into reality when I heard Timothy, one of my childhood friends from across the street, calling my name. We'd been friends since we were both six years old. When he ran up to me and began talking, I glanced over at my house and saw my stepfather in our living room window... looking right in my face. I pretended not to see him as Timothy asked me where I'd been. Even if I wanted to share with Timothy, I dared not do so now because I knew I was being watched.

After cutting our conversation short, I walked around the back of the house, slowly dragging myself up the steps. I absolutely hated going home. The fear of what my stepfather was going to do to me had the nerves on my spine feeling like they were crawling. Instinct told me that once I made it inside the house, things would be ugly for me. As I turned the doorknob to enter the house, my stepfather flung the door open, snatching me through it so aggressively that I fell to the floor. As I attempted to get back on my feet, he stood over me, unloading a barrage of interrogative questions so quickly that I didn't have a chance to say anything.

Uncomfortable, I kept quiet, careful not to lead Jim to believe that anything was going on between Timothy and me because I knew that would further anger him. Luck was on my side because his attention was redirected as we both heard my sisters running up the stairs behind me. I quickly gathered my books and bag from the floor and ran to my room.

Before settling in my bedroom long enough to exhale, my mother charged in behind me, asking, "Why do you instigate trouble with Jim? He loves you so much! He's taking damn good care of us... something that your father failed to do!" Without waiting for me to speak, she continued, "I don't know where we would be without him. He's told me how you tease him with your eyes, how you walk around the house with your breasts out and showing your ass! Jim doesn't want you, but you keep on enticing him. I'ma need you to stop it! Get yourself together! You are purposely trying to get his attention, but I'm telling you, it ain't gonna work!" she said, breathing hard.

My mother's accusations hurt my feelings. What she was saying was not true. "Ma, please don't believe this!" I begged. "You see me around the house. I don't have my breasts showing. I don't know how to entice anyone. You've got to believe me!"

Hearing those words, my mother rolled her eyes and walked away, refusing to speak or even look at me for the next few days. I'm guessing she didn't believe me by the way she treated me.

In the emergence of quiet, I asked myself again, as I had

many times before, *What have I done?* I couldn't think of anything I'd done to influence my mother's behavior towards me today or any day because I'd been in school all day. Jim attacked me before I could even get into the house good. My mother had to know this. I often wondered why she seemed so angry with me, in particular. She had begun to outwardly demonstrate her hatred for me, and there was nothing I could do about it. This is when I decided that moving forward, I wouldn't say anything to anyone, especially her, because I was too afraid to get the reaction I got from her. She looked at me with such disgust.

Knowing that my mother believed everything my stepfather told her, I tried as best as I could to be invisible inside our home because I wanted peace. I was afraid to even make eye contact with her and completely tried avoiding Jim. Whenever I was going to enter a room that he or my mother was in, I would quickly but quietly turn around and run back to my own room to avoid them both.

I desperately wanted to feel loved by my mother, and believe it or not, I wanted my stepfather to love me too... the right way—like a father should love his children. Sometimes, I pondered how different things would be if my biological father hadn't been an abuser who tried killing us. We'd all be like one big happy family, with my father taking good care of my mother, sisters, and me. Nevertheless, since my father was locked away in prison for the next fifteen years, that was not my reality. With everything we were going through, he couldn't protect us even if he cared because he was in prison for hurting us, too!

Instead, we were all here with this monster who cared nothing about any of us, including my mother. She just didn't realize it. As a result of her decision to be with Jim, we all suffered in some way. Knowing I was in a no-win situation, I would sit and consider ways to get my mother and stepfather to love me. Yet, nothing I tried ever seemed to work!

One evening, my mother saw my stepfather leaving my room. When he went into the bathroom, she stormed into my bedroom shouting, "You just can't help yourself, can you, Elizabeth?" Then she began beating me on my head and my face. Helpless, I curled up with my arms and hands covering myself. After she grew tired of using me as a punching bag, she ran to the bathroom where he was and told him to leave the house... *immediately!* I couldn't help but feel relief and guilt at the same time. Relief because she was making him go, and guilt because I caused her to put him out.

He collected a few items and calmly headed for the door. To my surprise, she quickly changed her mind, running ahead of him and reaching the door before he did. She used her body to barricade it to keep him from walking out. "You ain't going nowhere!" she shouted, begging. "You staying right here!"

Later that night, Jim came to my bedroom. He stood in my doorway, watching me with a smug look. My mother was on his heels. Jim walked away, but she came into my room glaring, telling me, "Don't ever have kids! If you want to be happy in life or keep a man, don't have kids! Kids just get in the way!"

I cried myself to sleep as I internalized her words, making a promise to myself that I would never have children, believing that children were a curse. Having them was the absolute worst thing a family could do. They would just bring about heartache and pain.

FIVE

MY BODY STARTED DEVELOPING when I was eight years old. Now, at eleven, I was fully developed and had even already started my menstrual cycle. Family members outside my home noticed how shapely I was at eleven.

One day, while next door at my grandmother's house, I helped her plant flowers and pull weeds. Even though she would take the liberty to degrade me and my sisters at every turn, constantly comparing us to her other grandchildren, I still loved her and treated her as such. While digging holes for the flowers, I told her everything happening in our house.

My gut had told me not to confide in her, but I thought I had to tell someone because I was desperate to be rescued and protected from Jim. It was either desperation or stupidity because I really wanted to believe that if I said to her that Jim was abusing me and now forcing me to sleep with other men, she would feel sorry for me and help.

She listened intensely, offering no comments. We continued to plant flowers silently, so I couldn't read what she might have been thinking. Finally, she interrupted the silence between us, saying I needed to stay out of the way. "You young girls these days are just asking for these things to happen!" she said. "Y'all just need to get somewhere and sit down. You're trying to be grown before your time." She concluded, taking this opportunity to tell me how fast I was.

While I was still at her house, she called my mother and told her everything I'd shared. That's when I heard my mother say that I was lying and for me to bring my lying ass home right now. Since I could hear her yelling through the phone, I just walked home, knowing I was in serious trouble.

When I arrived, my mother was waiting on the porch with the phone still in her hand. She glared at me as I walked up the stairs to our porch, swinging the phone at my face as I tried running past her. It landed, hitting me on my earlobe.

"I'm sorry, ma! I'm sorry!" I screamed in pain. "I can't take this anymore... Oh God! I just want to die! I want to die right now!" Bleeding from my ear, I ran to the bathroom crying. This time, I locked the door. I no longer cared if I got in trouble for it. Once the thought occurred that I better unlock the door, I was already prepared to run to my bedroom and bury myself under my covers.

From that encounter, my grandmother told everyone in our family how fast I was. She started telling anyone who would listen, which was everybody, that I was going to get a baby before I was eighteen. She would say, "I know she screwin' somebody 'cause she's built like a woman!" Her words, her lies about me, and her disbelief in me further diminished every fiber of my being. I just wanted to disappear into thin air.

My grandmother would say to me with disgust, "Yo ass is too big, Elizabeth! What are you doing to get an ass so big? You gon' fool around and get pregnant!" My grandmother had her share of supporters in our family. They would refer to me and my sisters as streetwalkers. She even remarked to my sisters and me, "Y'all gone be just like yo mother, house full of kids with nothing for a man! Y'all reek of welfare!" She and other family members treated us like we were trash. It disintegrated my self-esteem.

Since most of my mother's family felt like my sisters and I were disgusting, I didn't feel comfortable enough to confide in any of them. Since they talked so badly about my body, I became very uncomfortable with myself. Hating everything about me led me to look down whenever walking past a mirror. I would avoid my reflection because of the belief that I was an awful, disgusting person. My face, including facial expressions, my hair, and my body were all ugly. I picked myself apart from head to toe. Even analyzing the sound of my voice and the way I enunciated words had become commonplace. There was nothing good about me. I was disgusting!

Wearing oversized clothing was a way of concealing my

body and believing that my stepfather would leave me alone if he couldn't see me. In all my naiveté, I really thought that he would no longer bother me. I was wrong! I even believed that my family would stop talking about the flaws with my body. I was wrong about that, too! In fact, everything seemed to intensify. Now, all I heard from my family was that I was wearing baggy clothes because I had gotten pregnant.

Even though this wasn't true, it still hurt to hear it. I even recall walking down the street once. My grandmother beckoned me to come over to her house. At that moment, I hoped she would hug me and tell me something good about myself. Instead, she started pulling on my clothes and patting my stomach to see if I was hiding a pregnancy. When she realized my stomach was flat, she said, "I thought you were pregnant, Elizabeth!"

With my head down, I replied in a hollow tone, "No, grandmother, I'm never having any children."

She replied, "What kind of woman don't want no kids? It's something wrong with you, girl."

Walking back to our house, I felt defeated as usual.

* * *

I was a complete recluse by the time I had made it to ninth grade. I stopped talking to everyone. Being a recluse was easier because I could be in my own head. In fact, I kept myself occupied with my head down in a book, pretending to be reading. The truth was, I wasn't really reading anything at all. I was thinking... thinking about how I could get myself out of my situation.

Things started to change when I met my typing teacher, Mrs. Thomas, a middle-aged woman of about forty-five who was a sharp dresser. She always kept her hair and nails done and smelled like a flower bouquet. She was very outgoing and friendly. Mrs. Thomas would joke with the students in our typing class but drew a line that none of our classmates crossed because she was also very firm. For some reason, she liked me. I was usually quiet, not talking to her or anyone in my class.

Mrs. Thomas was the kind of teacher who let no student get away with being quiet. She called on everyone to participate in class. I could get by with C's in previous grades without digging in the trenches to learn and participate in class. And, because I was quiet, my teachers never pushed me to do any better. I was the one student who was able to fall between the cracks. Mrs. Thomas was different. She saw and pushed everyone.

At first, I was uncomfortable. It felt awkward talking because I'd taught myself to be quiet for so long and just go with the flow of things. I didn't make eye contact, talk, laugh, or smile. I was always serious, stiff, and more robotic. Even though I was always looking for someone to confide in, I realized it was better to keep myself closed off from the rest of the world.

One day, Mrs. Thomas held me behind after class. "Elizabeth, you have excelled in typing! You're a natural," she said. "As a ninth grader, you are already typing at a speed of 80 wpm. This type of speed is what employers look for. Moving forward, I want you to continue taking typing classes, and in your sophomore year, I want you to take my Gregg Shorthand class, too."

What Mrs. Thomas said felt like a compliment, but I hadn't heard a compliment from anyone in so long that I was working hard to process it. Realizing that I was confused, she repeated herself. "Elizabeth, you're the best student I have! You have caught on quickly to proper technique, developed skill, and used it to excel in typing. So, I want you to take Typing II next school year. In addition, I want you to take Gregg Shorthand. I'm going to make sure that I'm your teacher for all of those classes because I will mentor you, Elizabeth."

A lightbulb clicked. While still looking down, I slowly smiled, then became overwhelmed with emotion and started crying. Suddenly, I felt happy! I became alive with joy that I couldn't explain. This was all too much for me to process. I didn't even understand all of the emotions I was feeling, but all of them made me feel alive. At that very moment, I could feel loads of sadness, worry, and depression leave my soul, and I came alive.

"Did I say something wrong?" Mrs. Thomas asked, perplexed.

"No. I'm so sorry! I just can't believe what I'm hearing!" Through tears, I told her, "I'll take any class you tell me to! Did you say that you would be the teacher of those classes?"

"I'll be sure to arrange it so that I am, Elizabeth. I'll work with your counselor to make sure of it!"

Hearing this, I sprinted from my desk with a smile and, through my tears, said, "Thank you, Mrs. Thomas! Just thank you! I won't fail you... I'm going to make you real proud of me!"

SIX

As LUCK WOULD HAVE IT, I continued to do well in typing and now in shorthand, too! Mrs. Thomas kept her promise to mentor me. No matter what happened at home, I would jump up every morning to rush off to school. I couldn't wait to get to my typing and shorthand classes for two reasons: One, I was great at both, and two, Mrs. Thomas cared for me, and it felt good to receive kindness from someone who genuinely liked me. I had never felt this kind of love from anyone in all of my life.

Soon, I started to wish that I could live with Mrs. Thomas. This would be a way to escape my stepfather's abuse. At home, I would daydream about life with Mrs. Thomas, playing out what life would be like for me in my mind every night, especially whenever my stepfather would violate me. Eventually, I became a pro at mentally escaping his abuse because I learned how to banish my thoughts to a place where I was actually in a beautiful home with Mrs. Thomas as my mother. Thoughts like this helped me to endure many difficult times in my household.

One morning during shorthand class, I won a speed competition. I was so excited! I was given a mirror, a special pen for dictation, and a small bottle of perfume. Everyone was cheering me on. I couldn't believe my classmates were cheering for me; they knew I existed!

Outside of class, my classmates started acknowledging and speaking to me. I knew it was because we were in Mrs. Thomas' class together. Her class felt like a community; everyone demonstrated support for one another—spilling out beyond the classroom. After class, Mrs. Thomas held me behind to tell me that she wanted me to begin taking computer classes. She said that with my excelling in both typing and shorthand, it was time to learn how to operate a computer. She wanted me to learn software and data entry. This was all happening so fast, but I didn't resist anything Mrs. Thomas suggested. I had complete trust in Mrs. Thomas by now. As she was talking, my mind drifted.

"Elizabeth! Are you okay?" she asked. "Did you hear me?"

I snapped back to the present moment, shook my head, and said, "Huh? Excuse me? I'm sorry, Mrs. Thomas, I'm going to do everything you tell me to do!" I was smiling ear to ear! I was excited! However, just as quickly, I dropped back into deep thought and, out of nowhere, started crying uncontrollably.

Mrs. Thomas began tearing up as well. She asked me what I was crying about. My own fear was preventing me from telling her the truth about everything. I was afraid that my mother would get into trouble. I was worried that my sisters and I would be removed from the home and split up, never to see each other again. I was fearful that my stepfather would find out I told everything and then hurt my mother.

My teacher assured me she would protect me if anything happened. I continued to deny that anything was happening. She finally relented and said, "Okay, but if something is going on with you, Elizabeth, you have to promise me that you will tell me." I promised her that I would let her know.

On my way home, I naively thought, *I can't wait to get home to show momma what I won! She's going to be happy for me!* Well, the complete opposite occurred. As soon as I walked through the door, I excitedly shared my win and gifts with my mother. Instead of being happy for me, she rolled her eyes and told me she better not catch me wearing perfume around my stepfather. She snatched the mirror from me, telling me I didn't need one. "You already think you're all that! You don't need nothing else to make you think you're beautiful."

My heart sank as she was speaking to me so horribly. "Mom, can I please have my things back? I promise I won't even wear the perfume. I won't look in the mirror, I promise," I said, begging my mother to give me back what I had won in class earlier that day. My gifts were the only things I'd ever received that had such meaning. I had won fair and square and wanted them back.

After that day, I never saw my gifts again. My mother started wearing the perfume, which surprised me because she had told me that the perfume didn't even smell good. After a while, Mrs. Thomas noticed that I had not worn my perfume. After class, she asked me, "Elizabeth, you haven't worn your perfume. Why is that? I thought you would like it... and I don't see you using your pen in class. Don't you like your gifts at all?"

Now, I could no longer hold back the truth. Mrs. Thomas listened intensely, shaking her head with tears in her eyes. She couldn't believe what she was hearing from me. While I shared everything, she paced the floor, shaking her head in utter disbelief at what she was hearing. After I had told her everything, she reminded me that she was mandated to report it.

"No! No! No!" I said, panicking. "I'm scared, Mrs. Thomas! Please... No!"

Grabbing me and hugging me tightly, she promised to be there with me through whatever process I needed to go through. She proclaimed to me that I would always be able to depend on her. After apologizing profusely, she told me that she had to report this upon hearing everything because if she didn't, she could be putting me in even more danger than I was already in. She couldn't live with herself if she did nothing about this immediately. She then arranged with our principal for the rest of her classes to be canceled that day.

Sitting quietly, observing everything, I couldn't believe this was happening. Guilt and fear plagued me because I didn't want to break up my family. I just didn't know where we would all end up. What would happen when I got home later? What if the only person to believe me was Mrs. Thomas? I was a complete wreck!

Needless to say, things got worse before they got better. The Department of Health and Human Services was called to the school. They interviewed both my sister and me. They also visited my three younger sisters' school. They interviewed each of us. It turns out that all five of us unknowingly shared similar stories about what my stepfather was doing to us. Right from school, my sisters and I were taken into state custody— into foster care. My worst nightmare came true. We were separated, but eventually, we would have the opportunity to have supervised visits.

When the police arrived at our house, my mother was there, but Jim wasn't. They took my mother to the police station for questioning. She told police that all of her daughters were lying about everything. "They have never liked Jim. They've finally done it!" When Detective Carlson asked, "What did they finally do?" she responded, "They broke up our happy home. The worse one of all is that damn Elizabeth! She is always telling horrible lies about what Jim does to her! You can't believe anything she says! Her sisters are following in her footsteps because she has all of them brain-washed! This just isn't fair! You can't do this to my family!" She insisted that Jim loved us and took good care of us.

Upon finding out that we had been taken into state custody, my mother told police that she would never forgive us for breaking up our family. We didn't see or talk to our mother again for eight months. A family outside the city we lived in took my three younger siblings into their home for the next eight months... my older sister and I were taken in by Mrs. Thomas. My dream came true! I couldn't believe it!

I was so happy during this time in my life, but sad all at the same time because my three younger siblings were in a different home in a different city with a family I didn't know. Eventually, the state arranged for us to have visits. They were supervised and short, but I was happy we spent the little time allowed together. We spent all of our time together crying, hugging, laughing, talking, and comparing the homes we were now living in. My younger sisters didn't like where they lived at all; it was very crowded and not that clean, and the mother was mean and unfair. She treated my sisters as if she didn't like them.

The first time we had our visit, my sisters said that this family was taking in foster care children only to use them as maids. Their sadness was exasperated by the fact that the mother, Mrs. Eaton, and her husband created a long list of chores that included cooking for the family, washing dishes, and cleaning floors, windows, walls, and toilets. At the same time, they didn't make their children lift a finger. Their children would go behind my sisters and create a mess, then report to their mom that my sisters didn't clean the area designated on the list. This would anger Mrs. Eaton, causing her to yell at my sisters. Their children would mock my sisters afterward, teasing them for getting into trouble with Mrs. Eaton. Their children would pick fights with my sisters. The mom and dad would punish my sisters if they fought back.

Hearing all of this angered me and, at the same time, made me sad. I wished I could do something about it, but there was nothing I could do. The only thing I could do is just wait this out and hope for a better day for all of us. It seems my mother didn't care how we were all doing. While we were worried about each other, my mother didn't give a damn about anyone other than herself and Jim. This was so frustrating. I couldn't understand how anyone could be so blinded by love.

I loved living with Mrs. Thomas but didn't tell my sisters because I felt guilty about being happy, knowing they were unhappy. The conclusion of every visit was so sad. We would hold each other tight, knowing it would be a while before our next visit. We all promised each other that we would be back for our next visit, hoping it would be sooner than usual.

SEVEN

SADLY, we learned that our mother continued to deny every detail we shared with state and local officials about the living conditions in our household. Even though there was evidence shared with her by the state and local police, she denied that anything had ever occurred. She went on record saying that we were all lying and that she never wanted to see us again. It hurt so bad to know that my mother didn't believe us. She chose him over us, even saying that with us out of the house, she could finally start living as she always wanted. Having us got in her way.

Now, with all of her children in the foster care system and out of her house, she believed that she would finally have my stepfather to herself, making up her mind that she would terminate her rights as our mother. She went on record with the court that she no longer wanted the responsibility of mothering any children at all, now or in the future.

"The foster care system can do what they want with all five of you!" "I throw up my hands!" "Where's your father?" "He's gone!" "He can't help you because he's locked up." "He doesn't even love you all because he tried to kill all of us!"

Trying her best to rush the parent termination process, my mother's attitude in our hearings was evident to everyone. She was uncooperative, loud, and rude. We could feel intense anger from her. She had fire in her eyes as she scowled at us from across the room. Whenever she spoke, there were loud gasps in the room. I believe that everyone was baffled by her behavior. We were in disbelief, not able to understand why she treated us, her very own children, with such abhorrence and indifference. She advised the judge that she just wanted to be done with this case once and for all. The court system took note of her behavior in court and started the process of terminating her parental rights.

What my mother thought would be the time of her life was short-lived. During the time my mother was sure that she wanted to terminate her parental rights and live her best life with Jim, she found out that he was a convicted felon and had several misdemeanor charges against him. In other words, he was no stranger to the law. In addition, there was a current restraining order against him from one of his ex-girlfriends, Cynthia. She had a story very similar to ours. Cynthia and Jim had met at a nightclub, and their relationship continued while he was with my mother. He was living a double life. Neither my mother nor Cynthia had any knowledge of each other until now.

Though they were off and on with their relationship, Cynthia says that Jim was still regularly coming to her house to spend time with her. They were even talking about getting married. She told my mother that Jim was charming and romantic initially, but before she knew it, he had moved in with her. He almost immediately began beating her and her children. She described how Jim was breaking into her neighbor's homes, taking her twelve-year-old son with him, forcing him to commit crimes alongside him.

According to Cynthia, Jim had abused her sixteen-year-old daughter and tried to prostitute her. Unbeknownst to Cynthia, Jim picked her daughter up from school, telling her that her mother had sent him. Once she got in the car, he took her to a house that sounded much like the one he had taken me to. Cynthia's daughter, realizing what he was up to, fought for her life. She was able to get away and reported Jim to the police.

Jim was now hiding from the police for the crimes he'd committed before meeting my mother. From speaking with Cynthia and the police in such incredible detail, my mother began to understand that she was just a matter of convenience for Jim while he hid from the police; however, she still wasn't entirely convinced. I believe that my mother still hoped to be with Jim without any of her children. She just wanted it to be her and him.

There was one other woman who came forward to share her experience with Jim. Before all of us were removed from our home, she came to our house with a man she claimed was her husband, Nate, Jim's cousin. In truth, the lady was a woman Jim was messing around with, and Nate was *her* cousin. This couple came to our house many times. I remember it well. She went on to tell my mother that Jim had made her many promises he never kept, but she had thought things would change. Of course, nothing ever did, and she decided to give up on the relationship. Other than all of the lies he told her, she didn't have any stories of abuse.

After hearing from—and actually meeting the other women Jim was involved with, my mother decided she better sever ties with him because the story behind this monster never got any better. It was quite the contrary. I believe what helped her finally make her decision was hearing that the police had picked my stepfather up. Life with Jim, as my mother wanted, was now over for good. Police had spotted him leaving a drug house. They weren't even surveilling the house in hopes of finding Jim; they were posted up in the area to make a drug bust.

When he spotted the police, Jim didn't put up a fight at all. He simply threw up his hands and dropped to his knees. After making the official arrest, the police took him to the county jail.

While there, Jim called my mother. I guess he wasn't aware that my mother knew everything about him by now. He told her he needed her to get the money to bail him out of jail and get him an attorney. My mother began yelling at him about the other women. "Tell your other women to get the money for your ass!"

He responded in a nasty tone, "Bitch! I didn't call you to hear this shit! Get me the fuckin money!"

"How could you do this to me? I thought you loved me, Jim!"

"Bitch, I don't have time to talk about love," he shouted into the phone. "Do what I asked you to do!" and then hung up in my mother's face.

He didn't have any money. He expected my mother to pay his bail and obtain a well-known local defense attorney. Surprisingly, my mother refused to help him. She changed her phone number and never spoke directly to him again. The county jail is where Jim remained until the result of his trial sent him straight to prison.

We were told that my mother nearly lost her mind behind finding out about Jim's other women. She refused to eat and couldn't sleep. Both my mother and Cynthia had become friendly, talking off and on. Cynthia is the one to be credited for convincing my mother to get into therapy and fight for her children. Taking her advice, my mother spent the next few months in intense therapy. She worked through the trauma caused as a result of both the relationships with my father and with Jim. She spoke of feeling like a failure because she didn't realize that she had caused so much harm and pain to her children.

During sessions, my mother acknowledged the love she had for her daughters... including me. She even showed up for one of our supervised visits. We were surprised because she had purposely missed previous visits. The gifts she brought for us to the visit made us think it was only because she wanted to see us all one last time. She even questioned us about our foster homes, wanting to know if we were being treated nicely.

Our responses to her were quick and dry. As a matter of fact, our meeting with her was quiet and reserved. We saw no point in being happy to see her because, after tomorrow, we would never see her again. Once the time had come to close the meeting, my sisters and I cried and hugged each other as if we were never going to see each other again. We knew that we would probably be separated for good. When my mother reassured us that we would all be together again soon, we didn't believe her because we knew what the next day in court would bring.

EIGHT

Finally, the day had come. Today was the day that my mother would sign documents to terminate her rights as our mother. We had no clue what was about to happen. We didn't realize that our mother had changed her mind about relinquishing her rights as our mother. We didn't know that she had discovered such damning information about Jim and had stepped into the reality about who this monster was that would cause her to cut off ties with him forever. We didn't realize that she was in therapy to heal from her hurt and trauma. We expected that this would be the end of our relationship with her. We didn't want it, but she did, leaving us no choice.

It was a cold and dreary morning. Cloudy and dark outside, raindrops fell rigorously, streaming down the car's windows as we headed to court. Traffic was heavy because of the rain, and it was rush hour. I will never forget this day. I was entrenched in measureless thought as water from the raindrops spiraled down the sedan's windows. This was the most interminable drive I'd ever taken. We were due in court by 9 am. I felt like the weight of the world was on my shoulders. With every drop of rain that fell, the tears fell from my eyes, clouding my vision. I could not stop the tears from flowing. Every time I wiped my eyes, they watered again. Everything was a blur.

A lonely feeling of dread and despair filled my heart. I was afraid. Starring out the window, I focused as each raindrop hit the windows. I thought I would never see my sisters again because we would all be split up for good this time. To take my mind off the chatter in my head, I tried replacing my thoughts with thoughts of my typing, shorthand classes, and my teacher, Mrs. Thomas. Thoughts of Mrs. Thomas possibly adopting my oldest sister and me no longer excited me because we would still be separated from our other siblings. Even thoughts of what I most loved to do didn't erase my worry and fear.

Then I began asking myself, what if Mrs. Thomas didn't want my sister *or* me anymore? What if she only wanted one of us? Any way our situation turned out, we stood a great chance of being split up for good and, even worse, never seeing each other again. How I wished that I could freeze time. If I could just stop time, we wouldn't have to show up in court.

* * *

As we pulled into the parking lot, my heart was racing, and I felt butterflies in the pit of my stomach. My younger sisters were already seated outside of the courtroom. They jumped up and ran towards me and my oldest sister when they saw us walking through the door. Even though my sisters and I were reunited again, we were all sad and did not display our usual happy cavalcade of affection towards one another. My stomach was in knots. Finally, we were summoned into the courtroom. The state of Michigan represented us, while my mother represented herself.

Inside the courtroom, there was complete silence. There were spectators seated, observing and listening intently to our case. The room was dimly lit. The judge was a woman who reminded me of Mrs. Thomas; she had a soft face with a beautiful smile, but she was also firm! She seemed to care a great deal about our case.

Each of our state-appointed attorneys discussed our cases separately. While the judge was hearing our case, some of the spectators were gasping as they heard the facts—in disbelief that such horrible things could happen to children. There were some people crying and shaking their heads. The judge asked our attorneys if any of us would be speaking to the case. Each attorney declined. The evidence was damning, as the attorney representing me stated. Plus, at this point, my mother was here to terminate her parental rights. There was no need to prolong long the inevitable.

Now that it was my mother's turn to speak, I braced myself for what I believed would be my mother spewing out how she no longer wanted us. Surprisingly, my mother's demeanor and temperament reversed like night and day! Her attitude was loving, patient, and attentive. She listened intently. Just like that! A complete transformation! She began by apologizing to the court for her past behavior. Her eyes welled up with tears as she looked in our direction and apologized to my sisters and me.

Soon, she began crying so uncontrollably until her body became limp. She slumped forward, resting her chin in both hands. Then she put her head down. Through her tears, she continued to apologize. Once we all heard her say that she wanted her children back, all five of us must have all been thinking the same thing because, at the same time, we ran over to her without even looking at each other—hugging each other and crying uncontrollably. We heard the judge call a recess. When I looked up, I realized that everyone in the courtroom was crying.

The officials representing the five of us and my mother went into the judge's chambers. Before anyone said anything, my mother grabbed all of us, embracing us tightly. She apologized over and over again, explaining to the judge and us how much she loved us and needed us to make her life complete. I wanted to believe her in my heart, but I was afraid she wasn't sincere. I was trying to think about a motive for her to have changed her mind about wanting to keep us. That's when she revealed all that she had found out about Jim.

Everything became clear to me. I thought back to when he first entered our home. I remember the evil in his eyes behind his smile when he thought nobody was watching. I knew this monster was sinister when my mother first introduced him to us, but I couldn't pinpoint anything specifically. Now that we were listening to my mother give descriptive details about Jim's actions, I was in complete awe of what I was hearing. My heart ached for Cynthia's children... both of them. Jim had abused them as he had us.

After my mother took her time sharing every disgusting detail about Jim through her tears, the judge explained to her very sternly how she grossly neglected to keep us safe for so many years and reminded her how, just at our last hearing, she was sure that she wanted to terminate her rights as our parent. On her knees and through a river of tears, my mother begged for another chance to have us back, detailing how she was in intense counseling and had severed all ties and communications with our stepfather.

The judge looked at my mother without blinking an eye and asked my mother directly, "If Jim were not in police custody, would you still fight to keep him? Would you still be willing to terminate your rights as a parent if Jim were not locked up?"

My mother very quickly responded to the judge, "No, Judge! I would not fight to keep him. Please believe me! Over the past several months, I've had the opportunity to have intense therapy and do a lot of thinking. I realize the grave mistakes I've made at the expense of my daughters, and I'm working every day to forgive myself. I'll work even harder to make things right with my children, your honor!"

After what seemed like hours, the judge relented. My mother and sisters were grateful, but I sensed that my mother had an ulterior motive. I didn't trust her anymore. I loved her wholeheartedly, but my gut instinct prevented me from trusting her. After meeting with us for so long in the judge's chambers, it was concluded that we would not go home with our mother that day, but we would be granted a return to our mother's home in ninety days.

While staying with Mrs. Thomas, I felt heard, seen, and like she genuinely cared about me and my feelings. To be honest, I didn't want to leave. I wanted to stay with her because I was safe and secure; she was very protective of me and my oldest sister. The time spent living with her was the happiest; I was blossoming into a beautiful young lady, beginning to gain self-confidence and I truly felt like I could conquer the world while living with her.

Mrs. Thomas promised me that even though my sister and I were preparing to leave, we could always return if needed. She never stopped expressing to us how our living with her did as much for her as it did for us. She truly loved us and demonstrated it every moment we were with her.

* * *

Three months passed quickly, and we returned to court. The judge explained the terms in which we were to abide by. My mother was forced to file a restraining order against my stepfather; he was not allowed to be within 100 yards of anywhere we were. This would prevent my mother from taking us to visit him in prison if she ever decided that she wanted to be with him again. Also, she was required to continue taking a series of parenting classes and continue therapy for each of us, both separately and with the family together.

Therapy was a roller coaster ride for all of us. It was rigorous and included high and low emotions, but most of all, it was healing for us because it caused us to dig into our past and present traumas. My mother blamed herself for all of the hurt she had caused us through the years because of bad decision-making.

After about ninety days of therapy and parenting classes, my mother was ready to move us back into her home. She and my sisters were excited. Although I was excited, too, I still needed to move cautiously. Sometimes, my mother and sisters became frustrated with me because of how guarded I was—not as free with my emotions as everyone else. I needed more time to analyze all that was going on.

The night before going back to live with my mother was a long night for me. I didn't get an ounce of sleep because my mind was racing. The following morning, I took my time getting dressed. I dreaded leaving Mrs. Thomas' house. As we got into the car to head home, we started to cry profusely, hating having to say goodbye. Again, Mrs. Thomas assured me that we could always come back to her home if we were ever in need. She reminded me that we would also see each other every day in school—a reassurance that made me feel better.

Also, therapy would continue even after we moved back. I was happy because it was sort of a security blanket for me. I thought as long as we were in therapy, things were sure to improve. Still, I was extremely sad and afraid. I didn't know the future, but I would be cautious moving forward. I felt like the stronghold of support I had living with Mrs. Thomas was being removed right from under me.

NINE

My younger sisters were already home by the time my oldest sister and I arrived. Everything was different. Each room was painted bright white, and the walls held beautiful, colorful art and pictures of us—without my stepfather. My mother had purchased new furniture in every room, including our bedrooms.

Tiptoeing through the house, I exhaled a sigh of relief when I stumbled upon a new record player. I flashed back to the time my stepfather made my mother throw away our old one. Seeing all of the albums, old and new, gave me a feeling of nostalgia, happiness, and, believe it or not, a sense of peace. My mother told me to look through the albums and play one. As I began playing music, we started dancing and singing along with it. This was just like old times. We were back to the way we were before my stepfather moved in with us. For the rest of the night, we talked about old times and happy times. Nobody mentioned Jim at all. My mother ordered Chinese food for dinner like she used to when we were younger.

While we ate, we made plans to go skating, as we had done a lot in the past. It felt like old times. We were all excited. When it was time for bed, I decided to sleep with my light on. I needed to be able to see clearly just in case my stepfather appeared in my room. Even though I was feeling better about being home, I still didn't feel safe. It took me a while to fall into a deep sleep. I tossed and turned for a while at first.

When I woke up the next morning, my light was still on. I felt well rested. My mother heard me getting out of bed. She came into my room and asked me if I'd had a good night's rest. I confided that I was afraid and had kept the light on all night. My mother hugged me and reassured me that I had nothing to worry about.

Before leaving my room, she looked me in the eyes with an inordinate amount of sorrow and said, "Lizzy, I'm so sorry for everything you have been through." "I'm so sorry!" She promised me that I would always be safe with her moving forward and that she would never allow another man to do any harm to her family ever again. I wanted so badly to believe her. Only time will tell.

Eventually, we reunited with our friends. Word had spread that we were home, and our home quickly became the fun house again. We spent the rest of the summer as we had so many times before. Everything felt weird. I had to get used to the freedom that we had again.

* * *

Summer came to a fast close, and I was looking forward to going back to school as a senior in high school. Even though Mrs. Thomas was a phone call away for the whole summer, I hadn't seen her in a few months. Once school started for the Fall, I picked up my schedule and took my picture ID. I had Mrs. Thomas for Typing III, Gregg Shorthand III, and an intermediate computer class. The other two classes were required and not electives. I was delighted to realize I could spend my school days with Mrs. Thomas, who mentored me.

Senior year was a breeze for me. My confidence had soared, but I was still quiet, shy, and reserved. I didn't make any friends. Mrs. Thomas arranged for me to work part-time in the office as an intern for two semesters. I loved my new job. I was making money and was able to save and shop. This was exciting! I started buying scented lotions, perfume, nail polish, and many clothes. Beautiful clothes! I was even getting my hair done at the beauty shop now!

Mrs. Thomas taught me to save at least ten percent of every check. She also started talking to me about colleges as prom and graduation approached. I was too afraid to go away to college, so I settled on one of our local universities!

One day, as I was leaving my job in the office, a boy

named Jackson Timms came in asking for transcripts. After helping him, I discovered he was preparing to head away for college right after graduation. We'd seen each other around school many times but had not spoken. But while I was helping him, we began talking. I noticed that he was sticking around even after I'd given him his transcripts. As I was leaving the school's office for the day, he walked with me out of the building and asked if I needed a ride home. I was a bit afraid, but I decided to accept his offer.

We talked the whole ride home about everything. I was very comfortable with him. Once we arrived at my house, we sat outside in the car for hours talking. Our conversation was wholly innocent and platonic. I knew my mother would worry, so I asked him to come in to meet her. She seemed to like him as much as I did. By the time he was leaving, he grabbed my hand and asked if he could ask my mother's permission to take me to our prom. I accepted his offer, and so did my mother.

The next night, our mothers met to plan our prom. I was so looking forward to it.

* * *

Prom night was an evening of massive elegance! We took lots of pictures and headed off to a nice dinner at an Italian restaurant before going to the venue—a beautiful banquet hall mainly consisting of mirrored glass. The pathway to the main entrance was lined with pink and white lilies. There were gazebos in the courtyard and ponds occupied by ducks relaxing in the water. We could see ourselves in the mirrors as we walked up to the mirrored glass doors. I hadn't looked in the mirror at myself in years because I didn't believe I was beautiful. So, before today, there was really no need for me to see myself. I almost didn't recognize myself. Even I could not believe how beautiful I was.

As we made our entrance into the hall, we could smell the beautiful bouquet of floral arrangements that lined the walls. The melodic sound of contemporary jazz was playing throughout the building. There was a spiral staircase that led to a beautiful landing, just perfect for taking pictures. After taking a few pictures, we settled into our seats.

The whole evening was so beautiful. Everyone complimented each other. Nobody behaved like strangers. It felt good to be at prom—and to think that I hadn't even planned to go because I didn't think anyone would ask me.

After the prom king and queen were announced, Jackson and I left for a long drive around the city. We ended up downtown, where we decided to park, get out, and walk. We talked the night away. This was my first time being out on a date, and it was everything I'd imagined it to be.

Jackson was a real gentleman. He held my hand, looked at me in my eyes as we talked, held doors open for me to walk through, and periodically asked me if I was okay. After walking and talking for hours, we ended up back at the car.

We sat and talked for a few more hours as we stared out at the river glistening from the moon's reflection.

As the night came to a close, we headed back to my house and continued to talk, just getting to know each other. This had to be the best night of my life, and the memory of it would last a lifetime. My mother was still up as Jackson and I walked into the house. He thanked her again for allowing me to go to prom with him, and as he was leaving, he turned back to my mother and asked her if it would be okay for him to date me formally.

I was pleasantly surprised and smiled ear to ear. My mother looked at me as if she was asking what I thought. My smile told her everything she needed to hear. After he left, my mother and I talked briefly about my evening and then went to bed. I closed my eyes with Jackson on my mind until I fell off to sleep.

TEN

High school graduation was a very proud moment for me. I graduated and began college that fall, excelling in every class I took. Jackson and I were closer than ever before. Instead of going away to another state for school, he decided to attend one of our local universities. While I was in school to be a teacher, he was in school to be an attorney.

It was grueling for both of us, but we were driven and focused because we knew it would pay off. During college, I worked full-time as a secretary in the admissions department. It was a position that I enjoyed. It felt great to be able to fully utilize the skills I'd learned in high school to earn a great living while in college.

This position gave me a sense of self-worth because I'd worked hard to acquire the skillset necessary to fulfill my position while in college. I was forever grateful to Mrs. Thomas for mentoring me. She believed in me, so she continued to encourage me to put in the work to perfect my skill set. Now, I'm able to earn a living using those very skills that I learned because of her.

Jackson worked full-time in a law office as a legal assistant. He was learning a lot from the partners of the law firm he worked in. One of the partners began mentoring Jackson and helped him prepare for the bar exam. Jackson appreciated all of the mentoring he was getting. He was serious about going into domestic relations so that he could be a family law attorney. His passion was to represent women and children who suffered domestic abuse at the hands of their fathers and husbands. I cheered him on because of my personal experience, which I hadn't yet shared.

When we weren't working, we studied together. We also had our share of fun! and began planning a future together. I thought I was living in a dream. I couldn't believe I was as comfortable with him as I was. He was my first boyfriend! Jackson taught me how a woman should be loved and treated. He was chivalrous but assertive and tender, too. He opened car doors to let me in and out of the car, assisted me with sitting in chairs, and always let me in and out of buildings first. He believed in holding hands and greeting me with warm hugs and kisses on my forehead every time we got together. He checked on me throughout every day, and most of all, we had great conversations.

Everything we did when together felt natural. Nothing

was forced. As comfortable as I was with Jackson, I could relax, laugh, and be less serious. *One day,* I thought, *I should tell him about my childhood experience.* Until now, I hadn't even thought about sharing it because I had done my best to put it all behind me. I never wanted to consider myself a victim—an overcomer, but not a victim. As quickly as I thought about sharing with him, I put the thought out of my mind.

* * *

Our lives seemed to flow in sync with one another. Jackson was graduating from law school and had his test date for the bar exam. I was graduating from my teacher's program and ready to take my state exam to be a teacher. We had been saving money for five years to buy a home together. Things with us fell into place nicely.

Upon graduation and finally passing our state exams, we had positions waiting for us: Jackson at the law firm where he had worked since college, and believe it or not, I was lucky enough to obtain a teaching position at the school I'd graduated from. Mrs. Thomas was still there. I couldn't believe it! I was now working with my favorite teacher. I taught English Language Arts and creative writing for six periods to all ninth-grade classes.

Mrs. Thomas and I had maintained our loving relationship. I viewed her as a mother figure in my heart. I could never forget how she embraced me, made me realize I was beautiful, and instilled in me that I mattered. I loved being a teacher and formed relationships with all my students. I encouraged everyone's creativity and made sure that nobody was left behind. I structured my classes so that everyone was engaged in our classroom activities.

I loved my students, and they loved me. One student stood out to me, though. She was quiet, shy, and reserved. I could have easily overlooked her because she never talked in class to anyone. I noticed that she often stared off into space as if she had a lot on her mind. Her classmates never bothered her. For weeks, I observed her behavior; she would always complete her work, but she was distant, as if she had a lot on her mind. She reminded me so much of myself when I was her age. Then, I had a thought... I needed to make a connection with her.

In class the following day, she was her typical self—aloof —so I asked her to contribute her thoughts on a topic we were discussing. Initially, she was hesitant, and I could easily read her body language and facial expressions. She was uncomfortable. I encouraged her to go on and speak. She did. The culture I'd created in my classes was a culture of inclusivity. In my classes, students who usually would not have gotten along were now getting along very well and developing positive relationships.

This day, she spoke, but she kept her head down as she presented her ideas on the topic. Various students encouraged her as she spoke. There was something about this young girl; I continued encouraging her daily to engage with the class. I made her feel like her input mattered simply because it did. Day after day, I had to initiate her engagement. She was naturally withdrawn. She completed her work but always kept her head down and would always write or draw during class discussions.

One night, as I reflected upon the day at work, it was as if a light clicked on in my head. This girl was so familiar to me because she was just like me when I was her age. Then, I began thinking about my past childhood traumas and how I suffered the abuse I suffered at the hands of my stepfather. I started to cry uncontrollably because I could only imagine what she might be going through.

The next day, my students came into the classroom, and we went about our everyday activities. At the end of class, Lisa, the young girl, asked me if she could speak to me privately. I could see in her eyes that she had been crying because her eyes were swollen and red. We only had five minutes between classes, so as she began sharing, a group of students arriving early burst into the room, eager to get started.

"Never mind," Lisa said. "I'll see you tomorrow."

Now, I was on edge and worried about her for the rest of the day and night. So much so that I couldn't sleep.

ELEVEN

When Lisa came to class the following morning, she looked even more disheveled than the day before. Right before class started, she asked me if I could talk privately with her during her lunch. I promised her that I would make it happen. As promised, I arranged coverage for my class so that I could meet with Lisa in the principal's office. I was not at all prepared for what I was about to hear Lisa say.

Visibly shaken, tears flowed like a river as she began sharing her life of horror. She was just nine years old when it started. Lisa and her mom would visit her aunt, who was married to Calvin. All of the kids in the family loved Uncle Calvin. He was fun, light-hearted, and easygoing. He always played games with the kids in the family. He was a good listener, so everyone found it easy to talk to him.

The first time anything happened to Lisa, she was coming out of the kitchen. Uncle Calvin walked in as Lisa was walking out. He asked her to come sit down and told her how beautiful she was and that she was growing up to be a beautiful young woman. Lisa was confused and uncomfortable with the conversation. She got nervous when he asked her for a hug, knowing something was wrong. She was just unable to explain it.

That moment was interrupted when her Auntie Carolyn came into the kitchen. Uncle Calvin laughed as Lisa hurried out of the kitchen and back into the family room with everyone else. Lisa said she felt weird but never shared that experience with anyone else—not even her mother.

The next time anything else happened was when Auntie Carolyn and Uncle Calvin visited them. Lisa shared that he made it a point to pull her a little too close to him while hugging her. She could feel him rubbing her back, then he stepped away and winked at her. Still unsure about his actions, Lisa shared this experience with her mother, who shrugged it off as her uncle just being who he was and that there was nothing to worry about. Although Lisa still felt uncomfortable, she followed her mother's advice and shrugged it off as well.

Now, in high school, Lisa had fully developed into a teenager. One evening, Lisa's mother was called to work an extra shift. She told Lisa that her aunt and uncle were coming over to install a new garbage disposal. While doing homework, Lisa heard the doorbell ring. Looking out the window, she saw them talking about something, but she couldn't understand what was being said. Then, just as she opened the door, Calvin entered the house while his wife returned to the car.

"Where are you going, Auntie Carolyn?" Lisa asked.

Waving her hand, Carolyn responded, "Going back to the house! Calvin left his wrench... I'll be right back!"

"I want to come with you!" Lisa said quickly.

"No worries, hun! I'll be right back!"

Uncomfortable, Lisa went back into the house. Her uncle stood in the doorway as she tried to walk past him. Closing the door, he grabbed her, pushed her to the couch, and started ripping her clothes off. Screaming, Lisa fought with all of her might, which angered him, and he became meaner and more aggressive. Then, overpowering her, Calvin had his way. Afterward, he threatened her by saying, "If you say anything to anyone about this, I'm going to kill your mother... and Auntie Carolyn won't believe you!"

By the time Carolyn returned with the wrench, Lisa was in her bedroom with the door shut, and Calvin had already taken the garbage disposal apart. "Lisa... I'm back! Told you I would be right back!" Carolyn went to Lisa's bedroom and opened the door. "Are you okay, hunny?"

Lisa quickly walked over to her opened closet, pretending to rummage through her clothes. She responded, hoping to be as composed as possible. "I'm okay, Auntie Carolyn! Just getting my clothes ready for tomorrow."

Carolyn closed the bedroom door behind her, saying,

"Okay, dear, I'm right in the kitchen with your uncle if you need me!"

After Calvin installed the garage disposal, he and Carolyn left... with Lisa's aunt unaware of what had happened.

Lisa said she knew she needed to tell her mother and Auntie Carolyn; however, her mom was still working the extra shift, and her aunt was with her uncle. Lisa didn't get any sleep that night.

Later, after her mother had come home from work, she heard her coming toward her bedroom, which she always did when she returned home. Lisa desperately wanted to tell but didn't know how. Later, she would cry herself to sleep but was awake off and on until it was time for her to get up for school. She had to drag herself out of bed because her body was aching from trying to fight off her uncle.

Hearing Lisa's story, I was sick to my stomach. Filled with anger, sadness, and adrenaline, I called the principal and our school's social worker to come into the office. The social worker called Lisa's mother and the police—both arriving at the school within minutes of each other. In instances when schools call the police to report child abuse of any kind, the police automatically place the call to child protective services, which sends someone from the department to the school. In some cases, the children don't go home; they leave with CPS going right into foster care.

In this case, it was determined that Lisa's mother was not

considered a threat. In fact, as Lisa's mother heard her explain what happened, she became overwhelmed with emotions and began crying. While crying, she embraced Lisa, apologized, and wished that she hadn't brushed Lisa off when Lisa tried telling her about Uncle Calvin's advances before. Her tears turned into rage.

"I'll kill him!" she shouted through clenched teeth. "I'm going to kill him!"

She tried leaving the office, but the police didn't allow her, assuring her that they would handle Calvin and that she should focus on Lisa's mental, physical, and emotional health. Then, they accompanied Lisa, her mom, and the school's social worker to the hospital. In the meantime, a police car was dispatched to Carolyn and Calvin's home to pick him up.

As police were leading him away, he began shouting, "She's lying on me! Call my attorney!"

Carolyn, overcome with emotion, darted out toward Calvin, punching him in the face. The police grabbed her to prevent her from beating him further while they put him in the police car.

Lisa and her mom would later share everything with Carolyn, including the test results from the hospital visit. Carolyn didn't want to believe her husband would do anything so heinous, but she couldn't deny results from the physical injuries and DNA test results from the rape kit.

TWELVE

This was the beginning of a long journey for Lisa. It was all so surreal for me because I remember going through this very same ordeal like it was yesterday. I was grateful that Lisa had finally gained support from her mother and Auntie Carolyn through this very difficult time. In addition, I was there to support her, too. My sister, now a therapist, began providing intensive sessions for Lisa, who seemed to be moving through therapy smoothly, using the healing strategies she was learning.

One evening at dinner, Jackson and I laughed and talked about our day. I opened up like rain pouring from clouds in the sky without even thinking about it. Sharing with him the abuse that I endured, living in foster care, being separated from my mom and sisters, court proceedings, and all of the trauma that I experienced. Jackson listened intensely.

Noticing tears slowly forming in his eyes, I emphasized

to him that therapy was impactful for me. It helped me to heal myself and my relationship with my mother and to forgive my father and even my stepfather. Therapy revealed stored anger I had been reserving in my heart for my father because of how he abused my mother. The way I saw things was that if he hadn't abused my mother or attempted to kill her or us, we wouldn't have had to leave him. Then, my mother would never have met my stepfather, and he wouldn't have abused me.

Jackson expressed both sorrow and anger, but then he grabbed my hands, and while looking into my eyes, he apologized for all of the trauma I endured growing up. This discussion with Jackson was an intense moment that created a feeling of dread as I explained to him my fears about Lisa and the possibility that she may not have adequate legal representation. Without hesitation, he said, "We are in this together!" and then agreed to represent Lisa as her legal counsel, saying, "Don't worry, we have Lisa covered," before urging me to continue talking about my past. "Go on, sweetheart... tell me *your* story."

I spoke until I had shared everything with Jackson. It took him a moment to process everything. Assuring him that I was okay now, I encouraged him to ask me any questions he may have. Without blinking, Jackson looked into my eyes and asked, "How on earth did you ever get through that situation?" I couldn't even answer it, but I figured that while you're right in the middle of difficult situations, you don't even have time to worry, cry, or sometimes even feel the pain of the situation because you're too busy fighting through it—just trying to survive.

Instead of expressing my thoughts, I said, "It was very difficult, but I just knew if I spoke up to the right person, I would get the help I needed to get out of the situation. That person was my teacher, Mrs. Thomas. Now, I can support Lisa, as Mrs. Thomas supported me.

* * *

Going through court proceedings was challenging. While being reminded of my ordeal years ago, I was sick to my stomach hearing all that Lisa endured at the hands of her uncle. She testified how he had started "fondling" her when she was eleven years old and recalled the very first encounter.

Right after Thanksgiving dinner, while the rest of the family was in the family room playing board games, laughing, talking, and listening to music, Lisa was washing dishes. Calvin brought dishes in and put them into the sink. Naturally, Lisa stepped aside to give her uncle room to access the sink. But, when she tried centering herself back in the center of the sink, he grabbed her from behind, pulling her to his body, groping her breasts, kissing her neck, and whispered, "Girl, you're growing up!" Then, just as quickly as this incident had started, it was over. Calvin left the kitchen and went back into the family room where everyone else was.

Caught off guard, stunned, and confused, Lisa walked over to the kitchen table and sat down. As water and suds ran down her hands, she stared into space, instantly realizing Uncle Calvin's actions were wrong. Lisa's mother had walked into the kitchen, called her name, and found her sitting at the table with wet hands clasped together. "There you are, Lisa! Are you okay? What's going on?"

Lisa said, "Uncle Calvin hugged me from behind and grabbed my breasts."

"What! He did what?!"

Lisa explained that she became fearful that she would get her uncle in trouble. She didn't want her mother to be angry with him, and what if Auntie Carolyn thought she was lying? What if Auntie Carolyn became angry with her mom? What if this incident caused the family to break up? It was too late because Lisa had just told her mom everything. After hugging Lisa, her mom confronted Calvin, who explained that Lisa was confused.

This incident caused a rift in the family for a few years, and they had just buried the incident and started spending holidays together again when this last incident occurred. Now a ninth grader, Lisa was on the witness stand concluding her testimony, which was very difficult for everyone in the courtroom. There were gasps and tears throughout the trial.

After the deliberation process, the jury agreed that Calvin was guilty. Several months later, he was given a fifteen-year prison sentence. For much of the trial, Lisa had kept her head down. She never looked up because she felt shame, guilt, and fear. However, after hearing her uncle's sentence, she saw her mother and aunt hugging each other intently, demonstrating that they supported each other... and her. She began crying, relieved that she hadn't caused a family breakup.

Lisa's mom and aunt ran to her, embraced her, and thanked Jackson and me for everything. Before leaving court, I assured Lisa and her mother that I would support them in any way I could to ensure she healed and could move on.

AT LAST...

Later that night, I replayed the day's events in court, causing me to toss and turn throughout the night. I got very little sleep that night. As my thoughts wandered all over the place, I came to this conclusion: My biological father was still in prison for his attempts to murder my mother, myself, and my sisters. He caused us to run for our lives in the middle of the night in our pajamas, with bare feet. Eventually, my mother got on her feet but soon married my stepfather, who inflicted sexual, physical, and emotional abuse upon me and my sisters.

My mother and her family ostracized us and chose not to acknowledge that any abuse was going on at the hands of my stepfather. Our family was torn apart for years, with my mother believing that her children were her enemy. Then, I met that one person who heard me, embraced me, cared for me, loved me, protected me, mentored me, and continues to support me to this day.

Life was a boomerang. Everything I had gone through was challenging, yet I made it through. Now, my conclusion is this: I was able to help a young girl through the same ordeal that Mrs. Thomas helped me through. With those thoughts in mind, I closed my eyes and had a peaceful night's rest.

* * *

After everything finally settled, Jackson and I took the vacation to the Bahamas we'd been dreaming of. While there, we had the most beautiful fairytale wedding—a day that I will always cherish and never forget.

My mother, still single, is finally happy within herself. Although dating occasionally, she is contemplative about the choices she makes for those she dates. My oldest sister opened her own practice, providing therapy for children, and my younger sisters graduated college and created a non-profit working directly with victims of sexual abuse.

Mrs. Thomas and I are still very close, as are Lisa and me. She is now in college to be an engineer. Unfortunately, Lisa was only the *first* student I've encountered who was being sexually abused by someone she knew. She was not the last. I've been teaching for over ten years now, and it seems I meet young ladies every year that it happens to. While providing encouragement and support in any way I can, most importantly, I encourage victims to find their voice and *speak until someone listens!*

www.ingramcontent.com/pod-product-compliance
Lightning Source LLC
Chambersburg PA
CBHW060422090426
42734CB00011B/2404